# When the First A Changed My Life

# When the First A Changed My Life

*A Journey from Shame to Self-Belief*

By John Tenny, Ph.D.

Published by Learning Path Press

Copyright © 2026 John Tenny

All rights reserved. No part of this book may be reproduced, stored in a retrieval system, or transmitted in any form or by any means—electronic, mechanical, photocopying, recording, or otherwise—without prior written permission of the publisher, except for brief quotations in reviews.

First edition, 2026

ISBN: 979-8-9880537-5-0
Published by Learning Path Press

Printed in the United States of America

*For my parents, especially Mom—
for their patience, faith, and quiet encouragement
when I struggled to believe in myself*

*For my siblings: Mary, Rozanne, Red, Peg, Joe
for all their love, all my life*

*And for Grace—
my cheerleader supreme,
the one who always sees the better me*

# Prologue

Stories always start before the story starts. Before my time, my family had already survived the Great Depression, moving often to find work, sometimes quietly in the middle of the night. It was a family bonded by the struggle to find food and stable housing. My father walked to work with cardboard in his shoes so his kids could eat; my mother shared the last slices of bread with neighbors who had less. They went to church every Sunday, and being a decent person was more important than money.

The family had good friends. Marco, an Italian man from the old country, came every Sunday. He spent the day cooking the spaghetti sauce from the fresh ingredients from his garden while singing happy songs in his native language. He joined the family around the large dinner table, and the leftovers lasted most of the week.

As willing and able as my father was, work was scarce and often temporary. They paid bills as best they could, looked for ways to stretch what food they could get, and got by. "It doesn't cost anything to be kind" was a family principle. My father had a particular soft spot for the underdog, even while we were there right among them.

My parents never gave up, continually looking for ways to better the family and help others around them. Gradually, things got better. The food they ate had more protein; the first car was twelve years old, but they could afford the gas. The electricity stayed on, and the Christmas tree was bigger, with more tinsel than before. Laughter and love grew to match the growing stability. Money was tight, but not as tight as the bonds within the family.

It was then my mother said, with everyone sitting down for the family Sunday dinner, "I have some good news. We're going to have a baby."

## Chapter 1

Always the center of attention, my loving family gave me whatever I wanted. Spoiled? You bet I was, and I loved it. I felt like an only child, even though I had five brothers and sisters. Which happens when a baby comes thirteen years later, and your dad wants to call you Encore cause you weren't on the program. My world was full of fun, and early on, I learned how to get my way with my sisters; a few tears almost always turned things in my favor.

When we played catch, I liked to make a wild pitch to see my sisters run after the ball. One sunny spring Saturday afternoon, Rozanne and Peg said, "Come on, Johnny, let's play catch till suppertime." They tossed it underhanded, and I would get "Nice try" when I missed and whoops of celebration on the rare instance when I caught the ball. I made a return run-after-it throw, but Rozanne made a leap and snagged it. Darn! As she was about to toss the ball back to me, she glanced toward the house. "Mom is waving. Supper time, let's eat!"

We washed our hands and gathered at the table. Mom set a cold glass of milk by my plate and poured a teaspoon of Hershey's chocolate syrup from the small can into the glass. The spoon clinked as she stirred to dissolve the chocolate.

"That's not enough chocolate. I want more," I whined.

"No, that's enough!"

I started to cry.

Mary, my oldest sister, said, "I don't know, Mom, that's not very dark."

And Red added, "If they gave me that in a restaurant, I'd send it back."

A few more comments were made, Mom gave in, added more chocolate, and I stopped crying. I smiled at everyone and took a sip of the extra-dark chocolate milk.

Even at a young age, I dazzled them with my cleverness. Climbing on a chair, I helped my sister Rozanne do the dinner dishes. She handed me a cotton dishcloth and a dripping saucer. I wiped it carefully and set it on the towel on the counter next to the sink.

"Good job," she said and handed me another.

Then came plates, more saucers, and cups. The last item was the aluminum pot used to boil the potatoes. I asked, "How do I do this?" I knew how, but hoped she'd say she'd do it.

"It's simple. Dry it on the inside, then dry it on the outside. That's all there is to it."

A few minutes later, she turned to see how I was doing, but I had snuck off. I heard her going from room to room, calling for me. I waited on the back porch that cold fall evening, the cloth and pot in my hand.

Rozanne saw me through the window and snatched open the door. "What are you doing out here in the cold?"

I grinned. "You told me to dry it on the inside and dry it on the outside. So....I'm outside drying it."

Rozanne laughed. "You imp! Come on back inside."

The next morning, the phone rang. It was Grandma, making her weekly Sunday-morning call to hear the family news.

"Grandma, wait until you hear what your grandson did yesterday! We're still laughing about it."

I was nearby and strained to hear. That story got passed around among relatives and neighbors about what a clever little four-year-old I was. My mom was constantly telling stories about me to anyone who would listen. Praising me to my face made me feel special, but overhearing my family speak about me to others made me swell with pride.

It was fortunate that no one knew what lay ahead beyond home.

Home was a happy place for me from the beginning. Even before I was born, there was excited anticipation. My eldest sister, Mary, was a high school senior and signed up for the journalism class. It was the only class where students could use a phone. She wanted to be able to call the hospital to see if I had arrived.

As loved and pampered as I was, there were times when crying didn't work. One Sunday afternoon, I played checkers with my sister Peg by the upstairs window that overlooked the backyard. After losing my third game, I wailed, "You always win. I never get to win."

"That's right. I'm not going to just let you win. You have to beat me fair and square. If you want someone who will let you win, you'll have to find someone else to play with."

Peg tapped the board and said, "Don't jump the first one you see. Try to figure out what I will do next." We played a couple more games—and I won!

"Good job! You beat me all on your own." That burst of pride was way better than crying.

Red, my most doting brother, loved to cruise around town in his restored Model A Ford. I was in the garden catching the bugs chewing the green bean leaves when he honked the horn.

"Come on! I want some ice cream."

Always ready for ice cream, I jumped in the rumble seat, and off we went to the Velvet Freeze.

Red liked to coast down Woodson Road, the main street in town, and I enjoyed licking my favorite cone, black walnut, double scoop.

"Quick! Duck down. There's Jenny Karsten," Red said.

Crunched down on the floor, on one hand and my skinny knees, I quietly licked my ice cream while Red chatted with Jenny. But he was taking too long, and my knees were getting sore. Up I popped and said, "Hi! I'm Johnny, the handsome one!" Jenny squealed, Red laughed, and away we went, looking for another cute girl.

My family saw me as a unique person and accepted my developing personality as just what a child should be—in their eyes, I was perfect. The world, my world, was a place where days were fun and exciting, and every day a new adventure. Given that experience, I couldn't imagine anything else. Surrounded by adults and admired and loved from birth to age four, I was sure that all other adults felt the same. I knew I was a smart kid because everybody told me so. I knew that every day would be full of hugs, laughter, and uncomplicated joy. But then World War II arrived, and a small crack formed in that bright, uncomplicated world.

When the First A Changed My Life

# Chapter 2

World War II raged, and Red was in the hot spots as an Army Engineer. Since no one knew where he was or which battles he was fighting, the worry was strong and obvious. The family gathered around the wooden Zenith radio every night, twisting the dials to lessen the static and hear Edward R. Murrow's broadcasts. I played in the corner, absorbing every detail and hearing the family's comments.

Often on a Saturday afternoon, my sisters took me to the local theater to watch the latest war movies, and I got to see what I had heard on the radio. Afterwards, we walked home and talked about the movie and our favorite parts. That evening, I replayed the movie scenes with my toy soldiers. I followed the toy tanks around the alphabet blocks town, ducking snipers' bullets fired from the crevices of the couch. I didn't understand the difference between my pretend and the real fear that the adults around me were actually living.

One Saturday, Mary took me to see Destination Tokyo, starring her favorite actor, Cary Grant, and we shared the ten-cent striped bag of popcorn. At dinner, she spoke of how brave he was, how he had risked his life over and over. Mom quietly wondered whether Red might have been involved in that battle.

Later, I was in the corner of the living room replaying battle scenes when my mom said, "Johnny, put those away. It's bedtime." I tucked the soldiers in their cardboard foxhole, brushed my teeth, got into my pajamas, and went to bed. I had just fallen asleep when the nightmare began.

*Red and I crouched in a damp dirt foxhole that smelled like our garden when it had been freshly turned over. In the moonless night, the bright lights flashed as bombs went off overhead.*

*All around, we could see the muzzle flashes and hear the crack of rifle fire. I pressed closer to Red and felt his strong shoulder. I could feel him gently pushing back.*

*Then, out of the dark came an enemy grenade, landing at the bottom of the foxhole.*

*As I had seen in one of the movies, I jumped on the grenade, covering it with my body.*

*When it exploded, I could feel great claws ripping into my stomach.*

My screams brought the whole family to my bedside. On other frequent nights, battlefield dreams brought imagined injuries and pain and house-waking screams. Rozanne and Peg were always the first to reach me from their room across the hall. A couple minutes more, and everyone was there, lovingly competing to be the one to take me to their bed for the remainder of the night.

Those tight hugs were my protection from my own fear of war, protection the adults didn't have for themselves. I was warm and safe, snuggled up to my big sister, but my stomach still hurt.

My being a four-year-old casualty of war worried my parents, and they took me to see the doctor, a long-time family friend. There were no other kids in my neighborhood, an industrial area across from the Emerson Small Arms Plant, where mom worked.

"The war needs to disappear for this child," he told my parents, as he gently patted my back. "He needs to be around other kids as soon as possible."

I couldn't understand how war could disappear, but I'd be glad not to be scared every night.

From then on, there was no mention of the war by anyone in the family, and I was sent out to play whenever the war news came on. I never knew where my toy soldiers went, and Peg just said, "I put them somewhere, but can't remember where."

The next day, my mother acted on the doctor's advice. She met with the principal at St. Paul Elementary, the nearby Catholic grade school, desperate to find a way to ease my pain.

"He's having terrible nightmares every night and needs to be around other kids. Please let him join the kindergarten class. He can repeat it next year," she begged.

I started school the next day, mid-year, three months after my fourth birthday, and a year ahead of the required age of five. I thought I would love school, playing with friends, laughing with new people.

But kindergarten was the start of the anguish that would last throughout my school years.

When the First A Changed My Life

# Chapter 3

I always had a good time playing with my cousins and was excited to play with other kids. The evening before I started kindergarten, my parents drove me by the school to show me the large playground and the three-story brick building with lots of windows and a flagpole.

I had learned my ABCs at home through games played with my sisters. My 2s looked different, and I could never figure out the other way to make them. They always came out facing the wrong direction. Some of my letters were the same, but at home, it was never a big deal. It was just a funny thing I did differently. But in school, that resulted in my first shame.

The teacher, a tall and pretty woman who smelled really nice, had welcomed me with a smile and introduced me to the class. "John," (at home it was always Johnny), "sit there next to Robert."

She turned to the blackboard, with the alphabet and numbers across the top, and drew two squares. "On your paper, write how many boxes you see. Be sure to stay between the lines."

I had two pencils and a wooden ruler from home, but no paper. Heads went down, and pencils started moving across the room while I sat there wondering where the paper was.

"Robert, give John a piece of paper. John, you'll have to hurry."

I made my two and felt good about staying between the lines. But Robert looked at my paper and said, "That's not right."

"Yes, it is. There are two boxes."

The teacher arrived, tapped on my paper, and said, "Look at the number two on the blackboard. Does yours look like that?"

I knew something must be wrong, but didn't know what. To me, they looked the same, the number two, but with a red face, I weakly said, "No." She never said anything about it being between the lines.

She wrote a two on the left side of my paper and said, "Write five more number twos just like that." I tried, but by the fourth one, I was writing them backwards again.

Robert, tapping my paper, laughed and said, "Wrong again." Then louder, "Teacher, he's got it wrong again."

*Why did I do that? Why can't I do it right? Is the teacher mad at me? I bet she is. Everyone knows I did it wrong. They all can do it right, but I can't. I don't like it here.*

One sunny day in April, I tried to play hooky. As I walked the three blocks to school, I came to the small park with towering maple trees, the ground still covered in last fall's large leaves. I decided I would rather play in the leaves than go to school.

I was sitting in a pile of leaves when a woman walked by and asked, "Little boy, why aren't you in school?"

"I'm only four. I'm not old enough," I replied, smart enough to know that being in school at four years old was unusual and that I could get away with the fib. Unfortunately, a few minutes later, my brother Joe walked by and spotted me.

"What are you doing there? Come on, you're going to be late for school."

When we got to the school, he sent me across the playground to the side door. I tried to hide behind the metal stairs, but he made me go through the door to the room, where I struggled not to make my letters and numbers different from the other kids'. I didn't want to be different, laughed at, or scolded.

But here I was— thrust into a world that didn't know what to do with a boy like me.

*Why can't I do it like the other kids? Something is wrong with me. I want to cry, but the other kids are already looking at me.*

One evening in late spring, we had just sat down at the dinner table when my father said, "I have an announcement, good news. I got the job with McDonald-Douglas and we'll be moving to Overland. Better yet, Mom and I are buying our first house. We'll start packing right after supper."

There came a barrage of questions from my sisters: "What's the house like? Is there a movie theater nearby? Will I have my own room?"

My question was unspoken. "Will I have to go to school?" I hoped everything would be different there—but it wasn't.

Once in Overland, a small suburb of St. Louis, Mom walked me to All Souls Elementary, just three blocks from the new house, to enroll me in kindergarten. When the principal told my mother that the school did not have a kindergarten and that I would have to wait until the Fall to begin first grade, it was a shock since my nightmares had nearly disappeared. My mother passionately related my history with nightmares and the doctor's insistence that I be in school. She was persuasive, and I joined the first-grade class the next day, with the understanding I would repeat first grade the following fall.

The problems with learning that began in St. Paul's kindergarten continued at All Souls' first grade. My struggle to fit in, learn new rules, make new friends, and stay unnoticed went fine until it came to writing letters and numbers. Like the other kids beginning to learn to write, I had started out reversing many of them. The other kids figured it out. They got it, and I kept reversing letters and numbers. I still struggled with the number two. I made it backward every time. It looked right to me, and I just couldn't form it any other way.

This was the first inkling that I saw the world differently, that repetition didn't make things better, and normal for most wasn't normal for me.

As we approached the end of the school year, Sister Bernadette was teaching beginning math, simple addition. I was copying the math problem "two plus three" from the blackboard. One of the students had passed out rough-lined paper, the cheap kind that sometimes still had slivers of wood embedded in it.

With a thick wooden pencil in hand, I was doing my best when the teacher stopped at my desk and said, "You wrote that two backward again. Erase it and try again." Striving to be as neat as I could, I erased it and tried again. I stared at what I had written and was sure it was right. While erasing the smudged remnants of my first try, I heard behind me in a loud, exasperated voice, "Pay attention to what you are doing! That two is still backward. Do it over!"

I jumped, flushing with embarrassment.

I quickly started erasing again, only to mostly smear the soft pencil carbon and wear a hole in the paper. Panic flooded my mind.

*"I can't do it. It won't be right. She will be mad, and I'll get in trouble."*

I tried to rewrite the problem in another spot on the paper. I paused when I reached the two, staring at the paper, trying to remember how it was supposed to look, as one student walked by collecting the finished work of others.

I remained frozen in doubt and fear when Sister Bernadette stomped to my desk, snatched the paper from under my hand, and crumpled it up. "You've wasted enough time. You had better pay attention to what you are doing next time!"

Like the paper, I crumpled inside, a worthless piece of trash.

Even recess was a problem. The classrooms and playgrounds were segregated by gender, with girls on one side and boys on the other. A white line on the playground separated the boys from the girls. I had always mingled with my cousins, and it didn't occur to me to stay among the boys.

When the ball bounced across the white line painted on the playground, I ran after it. A gang of first-grade girls grabbed the ball and yelled at me to get back where I belonged. All the boys had to wait at the white line until they decided to throw the ball back, and then they blamed me for wasting our recess time. There was so much I didn't know. I didn't know about lining up, about raising your hand, about talking to the boy next to me, about staying in your seat. No one told me the rules, but everyone expected me to know them.

At the end of the year, my parents were surprised to learn that I would be starting second grade next year, instead of repeating first grade as had been arranged. It wasn't because they recognized some talent in me—the incoming class was already overcrowded. Another year of being the youngest, the smallest, and the one with the most problems learning.

I failed at St. Paul's, and here, in my new school, I was convinced the teachers didn't like me;

the other kids thought I was dumb. And worst of all, I started to believe they may be right. I wasn't just getting a number backward. I was becoming the boy who did everything wrong.

## Chapter 4

On a warm spring Friday, I walked the three blocks from my third-grade classroom to home for a lunch of a grilled cheese sandwich and Campbell's tomato soup instead of eating my usual newspaper-wrapped baloney sandwich at my desk. I enjoyed the quiet, cool kitchen, the bright sunlight spilling through the garden window—a welcome refuge after a morning filled with tension and confusion. After I finished lunch, my mother gave me a note for Sister James, the principal and eighth-grade teacher, about making girls' school uniforms as part of the cost of my tuition.

I went back to school happily, with the calm and loving home atmosphere fresh in my mind.

## When the First A Changed My Life

All Souls Elementary School was a solid red brick building, two stories high. The first floor held the auditorium and storage rooms. Inside the large double front doors, there were ten steps up to the second-floor classrooms. There, the Sisters of Notre Dame, in their floor-length black habits, maintained strict order and discipline.

When I arrived a few minutes before the bell rang, I went straight to the principal's classroom. At the doorway stood one of my third-grade classmates, pale and anxious. I said hi. She looked at me with teary eyes, and I wondered why she was there. When I looked across the room, I saw my teacher, Sister Salome, talking to the principal. Sister Salome was the oldest nun in the school, her memory and clear thinking already slipping.

In a few moments, they both stood and headed to the door. The principal took the girl's arm. Sister Salome pointed her crooked and knobby finger at me, leaning down close and hissed, "I told you you were going to get it!"

They marched us downstairs to one of the storage rooms. Without explanation, ordered us onto our hands and knees on the cold concrete floor and beat us with doubled-over rubber hoses as big around as a finger. It felt like it lasted a long time, and the beating left bruises on my hip and backside.

I had no idea why I was being beaten. I searched my mind, trying to remember what I might have done, but drew a blank. The note from my mother was still in my pocket. They never called my parents, and I was too ashamed to say anything.

To be honest, there were reasons Sister Salome might be mad at me. With my steady stream of rebukes and shame in front of my classmates when I couldn't learn, I developed ways to distract the teacher and stretch out the lesson. I made what the other students thought were funny comments; Sister Salome viewed them as disrespectful. I made paper airplanes to sail around the room just to get smiles from my friends. Launching those while her back was turned caused some commotion and got her to stop writing the assignment or lesson on the blackboard and take time hunting for the culprit.

Once, I got all the boys and most of the girls to push their books off their desks at exactly 1:30 by the large clock at the front of the classroom. The loud crash made the nun jump, and we all burst out laughing. She didn't and took some minutes scolding us. It worked—some academic exercise was avoided, and one less chance for me to fail.

Before that first beating, my disruptions were innocent; I was just being funny, trying to avoid embarrassment. However, after the next beating, my misbehavior became intentional.

My hate for school was matched by my love for baseball. After all, it was St. Louis, with the famous Stan Musial; my uncle Ralph had pitched the first major league game under the lights; and my Cub Scout pack leader was the sister of Yogi Berra. I played baseball every chance I got, interrupted only by the piano lessons my sister thought would be good for me.

At age ten, when I'd rather be playing baseball, I had my first piano lesson with Sister Anne at the convent. The Thompson Piano Lessons for Little Fingers were easy, and I did learn how to read the right-hand melody for those simple songs. However, as soon as the left hand was introduced, another facet of my learning appeared. I could not coordinate my right and left hands. I hated practicing, especially on a sunny Saturday when other boys were at the dirt lot across from the school, choosing teams and who would be the pitcher.

On one beautiful Saturday, I was scheduled for a lesson at 2:30. I left the house right after lunch and joined the baseball game at the dirt lot. When it was my turn at bat, I got a hit and slid into first base, forgetting that I was wearing my good pants and a short-sleeved white shirt. I also nearly forgot the time for my lesson and, at the last moment, grabbed the music book and ran to the convent. I arrived still carrying the dust of the game and sweating from the run on the hot and humid day.

When I sat down to fumble through the lesson, my dirty, sweaty hands were leaving wet fingerprints on the piano keys, and Sister Anne made me go wash my hands, scolding me for coming to the lesson that way. But even clean hands couldn't disguise the fact that I had not practiced and had not mastered the simple lesson. That really made her mad, and she grabbed my shoulder, saying, "I'll teach you not to waste my time," pulled me into the entryway, and pushed me to the floor. She pulled up the sleeve of her habit so that it didn't impede her swing and stuck me in a burst of anger, causing the dust from the first-base slide to fall from my pants to the floor. The shame was as bad as at school, that I had dirtied the piano and the floor of the convent, and that, at any moment, someone could come through the front door to witness my humiliation. I was a bad kid, and everyone is mad at me, no matter where I go.

*But if you're going to keep beating me, I'll give you a real reason!*

I started acting out on purpose, doing things to get back at Sister Salome.

I put thumbtacks and glue on her seat. I broke the points on all her pencils. On one warm spring day, the windows out onto the playground were wide open. I got out of my seat when her back was turned and, quietly climbing out the window, dropped to the asphalt playground. I walked around the corner to the school's front door and returned to class.

Sister Salome looked up from her desk. "Where have you been?"

"You sent me to the office with a note."

"I did?" she said, obviously confused. "Okay. Take your seat."

Nearly every day, she would say that I had to stay after school to write "I will not shoot spit wads" one hundred times or read aloud some passage I had stumbled over in class. Many times, I was made to dust erasers and clean up the classroom while being scolded for my transgression. But most days, when we lined up to leave, I would get in line and walk out the door with everyone else. Sister Salome never seemed to remember telling me to stay after school. She probably just didn't want me around.

*I don't want to be the bad kid. I want to be a good kid, but I don't know how to make you like me. I can't do what you want me to, but I try! I don't know why I can't remember the names of planets or the seven times table. I don't want to disappoint anyone. Help me. Show me what to do.*

In spite of the hour of practice every day, timed by my mother, I struggled to learn to play the piano. When the public recital came around six weeks later, I still couldn't get the two hands to work together—my mind couldn't process that complexity.

The crowd of parents and families filed into the hall and found seats among the wooden folding chairs. I was incoherent with fear, and when my turn came, it took all my strength to walk up the steps to the stage and move to the grand piano. With trembling hands and awash in shame, I made mistakes, started over with more mistakes, and just quit halfway through the piece.

When I got up to take my bow, the only face in the crowd I saw was my mother, and her disappointment and embarrassment. I had publicly shamed not only myself but also the person who had always loved me the most.

*Mom, I'm sorry. Please don't give up on me. I tried. Everything seems so hard for me.*

I never had another piano lesson, and for years, every time I walked through the living room and saw that piano and the empty bench, it renewed my sense of failure.

Third grade made my learning problems more obvious. In the mid-1940s, learning the times tables by third grade was a significant goal. No matter how many times we recited in unison as we marched to lunch, it never stuck for me.

*I couldn't memorize the presidents' names, the dates they served, or when the battles were fought. Those isolated bits of information vanished the moment I shut the book.*

Memorizing lists of names and dates, usually alphabetized to help when we had to look them up in the dictionary, for me were mostly just another barrier. Something I just knew I couldn't do because I'd never been able to do that, even from first grade.

I tried, but I just couldn't do what they demanded of me: reading and memorization, and math. I would be embarrassed every day at school, terrified when it was my turn to read aloud and show everyone I couldn't get it right. Or work on a problem on the board, my mind always a whirlwind of confusion and dread. But it was really report-card time that it became public as I brought the shame home.

Those were the days when they gave grades for academics and commented on your deportment. There were comments on paying attention, getting along with others, being polite, being responsible, and making an effort. I still have the report card with the comment, "He works harder to get out of work than if he just went ahead and did it."

From first grade on, comments included, "He is easily distracted," but mostly it was just, "He doesn't try hard enough." Those report card comments further drove home that something was wrong with me. I wanted to do what other kids did, but I never could figure out how to do it.

When they saw me staring off into space and viewed me as distracted or daydreaming, it was me juggling the ideas to get them in an order I could understand.

Jerry Roberts was a friend and a classmate, and he got top grades and praise from the teacher. When he stood to read the word problem in the math book, he sounded smooth and confident. When I read, my voice was shaky, and I couldn't pronounce the long words. His work got held up to show the class how it should be done; mine never did.

My mother said, "You're every bit as smart as Jerry Smith. You know that, don't you?"

*"If I'm as smart as he is, how come I don't get the same grades that he does? It's not fair that it's easier for him. I should get to be as good as the other kids, but the teacher doesn't like me."*

Once, in a conversation about how unhappy I was at school, my mother said, "You are just different from the other kids."

"I don't want to be different! I just want to be like the other kids," I cried, my eyes full with tears of anger and resentment.

*I can't learn, and I hate school! Isn't there somewhere where I can be okay?*

# Chapter 5

In February of my fifth grade, I joined the Boy Scouts and found a world that ignored my school history and taught through hands-on activities. When I attended meetings, I learned about knot tying, life-saving first aid, and that I should help little old ladies across the street. Here, I could demonstrate my learning to other Scouts and the leaders, gaining recognition and acceptance.

When we went on a weekend camping trip, I learned to be clean and helpful, and to leave the campsite better than we found it. I could tell stories around the campfire or show new scouts how to start a fire with just one match. It was a replica of home's atmosphere in a new setting with new people. It was fun; I got to learn and teach, be the kid who knew things, and no one knew that, at school, I was a stupid failure. I had found my first place away from the shadow of the classroom.

With the room crowded with parents and scouts, the Scoutmaster, master of ceremonies, stepped to the podium. "We are here to award merit badges to scouts to have demonstrated knowledge, skill, and personal growth in many areas. Each badge represents new understanding gained, challenges overcome, and solid learning."

When he said, "John Tenny, you have earned merit badges in First Aid, Cooking, and Citizenship. Congratulations, " I had a moment of pride and recognition for what I had learned.

*Could I be smart in one place and dumb in another? How could that be?*

A week into sixth grade, two boys, Ken Rose and Mike Anello, joined our class. At lunch recess, several of us were shooting baskets, and Ken and

Mike stood on the sidelines watching. When the ball bounced my way, I said, "Your turn," and tossed the ball to Ken. He took a shot, and the ball bounced off the rim. Mike stepped in, caught the ball, dribbled a couple times, and made a nice hook shot.

The ice was broken, and when school let out, we walked together and talked about nothing in particular except baseball and where we lived.

*Could I reinvent myself with them?*

They were regular guys—sometimes neglecting to do homework, sometimes staying after school to wipe the chalkboard and dust the erasers. I could make friends with them because they hadn't witnessed the five years of my failures.

Mike's mom was a lively Irish redhead married to an energetic dark-haired Italian, and the house was full of laughter. Ken's mom seemed to always be in the kitchen. Most important was that she made the best chocolate chip cookies.

## When the First A Changed My Life

I once told Ken, "You know I don't really like you. I just hang around cause your mom makes such good cookies."

He told his mom I said that, and we got even more cookies. I not only had my friends but also other adults who liked me, who didn't care, or maybe didn't even know about how I was at school.

Ken and Mike came to my house on a summer Saturday to spend the night. We spread blankets on the covered front porch, just outside my parents' bedroom. When we were sure they were asleep, we quietly rolled our bikes down the hill. We spent the next hour or so cruising the quiet night in our small town, the cool night air a relief from the hot, humid day.

We never got into any mischief or bothered anyone; we just roamed freely and talked, accepting and without judgment. Like the Boy Scouts, here I was safe from ridicule, and I could be the calm and confident kid I wanted to be.

*I wish school was like this.*

One afternoon, Ken, Mike, and I were on our bikes and stopped at a stop sign when a couple in a car stopped next to us.

"Can you tell me how to get to city hall?"

I said, "Go two blocks straight ahead, turn right for one block, then left. In about three blocks, you'll see a large brown building on your left. That's it."

When they had driven off, both Ken and Mike looked at me in amazement.

"City Hall isn't that way!"

I laughed, "Right—but they don't know that."

I got to be funny and never said, "I don't know."

It wasn't easy to shake the impacts of constant failure at school. Lying became a main defense tool in any situation. I had said, "I don't know," so many times in class and been ridiculed or yelled at that I avoided ever sounding like I didn't have an answer.

I was the youngest in the class and could have been the model for the 98-pound weakling on matchbook covers advertising the Armstrong Body Building course. I needed something to fend off the bullies, so I complimented them on their strength, poked fun at myself, and remained non-challenging. I could talk my way out of almost anything.

"I'm going to bust you in the mouth."

"Hey, you're bigger than me, stronger and faster than me. Hitting me would be a waste of your time."

"You're a stupid shrimp."

"Yeah, that's what the butcher says."

Disgusted, he turned and walked away.

Those skills—and the lying I relied on—worked with adults, too. I knew it was fake, that I was just a kid who really didn't know anything, hiding my failures.

Outside of school, I could cover it up, but I still knew.

The three of us stayed close through eighth grade, and then starting high school took us in different directions. Ken and Mike went to a public high school, while I began my freshman year at a boarding school in Carthage, Missouri. I will miss being separated from my accepting friends.

When the First A Changed My Life

## Chapter 6

Our Lady of the Ozarks was a Catholic seminary that began the path toward priesthood, another effort by my parents to help me learn. They hoped the strict, focused atmosphere might make a difference.

It was another act of love that didn't work out. It actually was worse.

Away from home for the first time was an exciting and scary adventure. Dad bought me a portable typewriter and painted my name in bold white letters on a trunk that was to be at the end of my bunk bed. I had packed my favorite T-shirts and my baseball glove. In the trunk were also two new white dress shirts, one of Dad's ties, and my first sport coat, a required part of the seminary attire.

My grandmother came along with my folks for the 300-mile drive to deliver me to Our Lady of the Ozarks for the start of a new school year. As they got ready to go, she said to my mother, "He's such a crybaby, he won't last a half hour." But she was wrong. I was glad to be here, away from my past.

I couldn't wait for them to leave. As I was saying goodbye, I could see several boys on the baseball field. I was anxious to join this group of kids that didn't know me, didn't know my history. I was once again at a new school with new teachers and new kids.

*Maybe I can learn here.*

As much as I anticipated a new beginning, it didn't last. The classes were harder, the teachers stricter, and the cascade of assignments more intense. It quickly became clear to everyone that memorizing the biology terms or translating Latin was beyond me. The same looks of disdain and smirks from students appeared quickly, along with

"You'll have to do better" from the teachers. I didn't even have a way to walk home from school—it was my entire life now.

My defenses reappeared just as quickly. I promptly became known for making everyone laugh, with students more than teachers, and for the harmless distractions that took time away from classes.

On a sunny fall day, we all had been outside enjoying the mid-morning break. When the bell rang, and we gathered to go back to class, I thought it would be funny to march in with our pants legs tucked into our socks. Somehow, I managed to get everyone, all 90 students, to follow me, stepping harder than needed, back to class two by two. It took up ten minutes of class to get everyone settled down—ten minutes of no teaching, no embarrassment.

The second floor of the stone, castle-like seminary building held the dormitory. Metal lockers separated six double bunk beds. Lights-out and no-talking rules were strict and uniformly observed.

In the evenings, students took turns playing at the five ping-pong tables in the gym. Occasionally, a ping-pong ball would get cracked and discarded. They would still bounce a little, but not good enough for play.

I collected a couple of those, and that night, after lights out and all was quiet, I tossed one over the top of the lockers from my top bunk bed. When I heard the boing, boing, boing as it bounced along, I smiled. A few minutes of silence, when the bouncing ball began again, tossed by another student. This continued, student to student, until the dorm proctor said, "OK, that's enough!" and the sound of giggles rippled across the dorm.

Somehow, the teachers found out, or perhaps just expected me to be the culprit, and for a short time, they called me "Ping-Pong." Fun little pranks were the only way I knew to survive. Teaching continued to be the stream of facts to remember, the vocabulary lists in science, and dates in history to balance, all mental tasks outside of my Boy Scout successes of actively doing something.

Students were only allowed to leave the campus on Sunday afternoons, and a map was posted showing the boundaries of where we could roam. I heard from a town kid that there was an abandoned quarry outside of town that was great for swimming.

One warm spring Sunday, the noon bell signaled that we could head to town. I was standing with about ten other students, and said, "How about going swimming? I know a place just out of town where we can swim."

"That's outside the boundary, and we can't go."

"Sure, we can," I assured them it would be fun, that we wouldn't get caught, and that it wasn't far outside the border.

After a twenty-minute walk, we found the quarry, tossed in some rocks to scare off snakes, and spent the next hour laughing, splashing, and jumping from the high spot on the bank. After a solemn promise not to tell anyone, we slipped back to school like nothing had happened. I never thought of myself as a leader, just a kid with ideas, but others did.

The seminary fed us well, if mostly plain food. Often, we would get a small red delicious apple with our lunch sandwiches. Taking food outside the dining hall was not allowed. But one day at recess, I said, "Hey, everybody, tomorrow let's sneak the apple out, and we'll pile them on the teacher's desk. You are supposed to give an apple to the teacher, right?"

The next day, there was a pile of apples on Father Robert's desk when he came in. His mouth actually flew open, then he smiled, then he frowned, probably thinking about our rule-breaking and what he would do with all the apples. And whose idea was it in the first place.

"Thank you all for the gift of these fine apples, more than I can eat. John Tenny, would you gather the apples and give one to each student? You can eat them in class," he said with a smile. The class laughed and cheered.

His smile vanished, and he said sternly, "But don't do it again." Looking directly at me, he said, "You all know the rule about taking food out of the lunchroom." The class got still, and we all felt guilty as we quietly ate the apples.

*Why did he have me pass out the apples? How could he know it was my idea? Did he think it was funny, or is he really mad? Now I'm probably in trouble.*

*And I was.*

Two days later, Father Martin, the school principal, charged into the room, the first time in the entire school year. His flowing black cassock swept behind him.

"I have a very important message for you, and I want your full attention." All motion stopped, and the only sound was the hissing of the steam radiator.

"There has been a surge of class disruptions—pranks that are not funny and rule-breaking. It has to stop!"

My face flushed. I knew.

He then pointed directly at me and forcefully said, "Do not follow John Tenny! He is leading you in the wrong direction. If you take part in any of his shenanigans, you will become the kind of person not suited to be a student at this school."

He paused.

"If he spent his energy on learning instead of being disruptive, he would be doing better in his classes."

"I'll say it again – do not follow John Tenny."

I stopped breathing, my face burning, and I stared open-eyed, not believing this was really happening.

*I crumbled, shattered, dissolved into the most broken little boy. I had been shamed many times for not knowing, but never for just being. I always struggled to find others who liked me, and this is the end of all that. Now nobody, no teacher, no student, will like me.*

*Am I really a bad person? Can you be a bad person and not even know it?*

In the past, I had rebelled over unjust punishment; now I just withdrew. I became small, disappearing, wishing I were invisible. I couldn't look at anyone; I had lost my voice and my laughter.

At mealtimes, students at my table ate silently, not looking up from their plates. Even Tommy, who sat next to me, turned away when I tried to talk to him. No one approached me outside of class, and I stayed away from everyone. In class, I didn't have the energy to be engaged.

"Tenny," the teacher said, calling on me in the mythology class, "What is the name of the Roman god of war?"

With eyes on my desk, I shrugged my shoulders. I knew it was Mars, but I couldn't say it.

I just shook my head. I couldn't speak; I had nothing left.

Near the end of the school year, I was called to the principal's office. "After careful consideration, we have decided that it's best that you not return next year." Finally, it was over.

I packed my trunk well ahead of the last day of school. On that blustery spring day, with the sun coming and going as the clouds whisked by, I watched my trunk slide into the bottom of the Greyhound bus. I released the deep breath I had been holding since that shameful day. I took my seat and escaped.

They might have helped focus my leadership talents, or looked for signs of my successful learning—but they didn't. Could they not see that there was a reason behind my pranks?

As the bus climbed the southern Missouri hills, I wondered if whatever awaited ahead would be any better—or just more disgrace and humiliation. Was I ever going to figure out what was wrong—with me, or with the world around me?

# When the First A Changed My Life

## Chapter 7

After scraping by year after year, I finally graduated from Mercy High School, ranking 281 out of 315, in the bottom 10%. It was a close call whether I would graduate at all. I flunked a couple of classes during my junior year and had to go to summer school to make up the credits.

The English Literature teacher sat us in alphabetical order and was the worst possible teacher for me. She believed that memorizing passages from great literature was critical to a good education. She would assign a portion of a famous text, and we were expected to memorize it overnight. She would start at the beginning of the alphabet, and each student, in turn, would stand and recite the passage. The following day, she would start from the end of the alphabet.

Terry Doherty was a buddy who was more interested in girls than school. He and I were fourth from our respective ends of the alphabet. We made a pact never to memorize it as homework, but only to listen to the three who came before us. A fun contest, one that I knew I would lose.

It had always been impossible for me to memorize anything, no matter how hard I tried. Terry passed, and I didn't, and off to summer school I went.

Summer school was at a public high school where none of the teachers knew me. One day in mid-July, when I left the first-floor class, I put my glasses in my pocket. Just as the bell rang, I went up to the teacher in the second-floor class and said, "Mr. Moore, I've left my glasses in the classroom downstairs."

"OK, go get them. But you have three minutes to get there and back."

"No problem. I'll hurry."

I left the room, walked to the far end of the hallway, lit a cigarette, and stuck the fuse of a cherry bomb firecracker in the end. I quickly hid it behind the radiator at the end of the hall, put my glasses on, and hurried back to the classroom. I didn't know it, but that radiator was right outside the chemistry lab.

The loud boom, echoing up the hallway, made everyone jump. The teacher looked down the hall, saw the cloud of smoke, and pressed the fire alarm. All the classrooms rushed for the exits.

In the distance, sirens sounded, and the fire trucks arrived, followed by two police cars. Firemen rushed in, hoses strung out, administrators and janitors ran around the outside of the building searching for stray students.

Shortly, school buses arrived, "School is cancelled for the day. You will be notified about tomorrow after the damage has been assessed."

Mission accomplished.

They questioned a couple of other students, but not me—I had returned to class seven minutes before the blast. I enjoyed the day off and never told a soul. Not even my best friend.

In my senior year, I passed a biology class with the solemn promise that I would never take another Biology class. Maybe if the lessons had been more about the concept of the circle of life instead of a test on the body parts of the dissected frog, I would have done better.

I had skipped so many classes in the required Civics class that the teacher thought I had dropped out. He passed me with a D-minus. A few teachers commented on my complex thinking during class discussions and on how quickly I saw the big picture, even as I scored low on tests and neglected homework.

Somehow, I'd made it, but I didn't belong among the real graduates. I felt like a fraud walking across that stage.

After high school, I enlisted in the Coast Guard for a six-month active-duty program, followed by seven and a half years of weekend training. As part of those six months, I was assigned to a ship cruising to Bermuda. Aboard, I was given various tasks to maintain the ship.

Two other reservists and I got the job of waxing the sleeping quarters floor—a floor that had been covered in multiple layers of yellow wax.

The typical routine was to sweep the floor and mop on another coat of wax as quickly as possible. I thought the floor looked terrible, dingy and old.

"Why don't we do this right?" I said. "Scrape this old wax off and start from fresh."

They agreed, and we went to work on our hands and knees, chipping away at the built-up wax. After a few minutes, we could begin to see the original flooring, a bright pattern of colorful triangles.

Somewhere in that sweat and mess, I realized: I was leading. I had set a positive goal, and both of my co-workers followed suit. I didn't shout or command, but lead—and they were following. But I kept remembering "Don't follow John Tenny." *Should I have just kept quiet?*

Late in the day, the Chief Petty Officer walked in. He stopped cold. "What the hell? This floor has not looked like this in the ten years I've been aboard this ship."

There were still a couple of feet to go, and the contrast was glaring

Turning to me, he said, "It's quitting time. What do you want to do?"

Without looking at my co-workers, I said, "You keep people out of here. We'll finish it. And be sure we get something to eat."

"You got it!"

We finished in another couple of hours while the rest of the ship ate beef stew and carrots for dinner. When we reported to the mess hall, steak and baked potatoes were waiting for us. The cook said, "What did you guys do, save the Chief from falling overboard? These steaks came from the officer's locker."

A job worth being proud of, and I had led two other hard workers into doing it. For a brief moment, I wondered if maybe I was good at something. But I wasn't running toward something. I was running away, looking for a world that didn't know me.

I returned home at the end of the six months, arriving in early May. Right away, my mother sat me down to talk about what I would do next. Since she had an unwavering belief in my capabilities, college came up as an option.

As she went down the list of possible careers, she asked, "Do you want to be a doctor?"

"No"

"Would you like to be a lawyer?"

"I don't think so."

"How about a teacher?"

"No! I could have a whole class of students like me!"

I joked, but it wasn't funny. I couldn't imagine being the person in front of the class when I'd barely survived being the one hiding in the back row.

I didn't want to go to college, but I was the youngest of six kids, and neither my parents nor my siblings had been able to attend college. They grew up during depression times, when it just wasn't an option. I was the hope for the family.

Further down the list was Funeral Director/Undertaker, and I thought, "I don't know anyone who does that." I recognized the first choices as academic topics, but I thought maybe the funeral business wasn't. I wanted to pick something, anything, that didn't feel like a test I was bound to fail. The idea of the funeral business wasn't thrilling—but it didn't come with essays, formulas, or Latin vocabulary.

My mother called the local funeral home and arranged for me to watch them embalm a body. A week later, I got a call saying that a woman in her thirties had died. I went to the funeral home the next day. I stood for several minutes outside, nervous about seeing a dead person for the first time. Taking a deep breath, I knocked on the door.

The embalmer, an older man dressed in jeans and a short-sleeved shirt, opened the door.

"So, you are the young man who wants to be an undertaker. We don't usually do this, but follow me. The embalming room is at the back of the building."

As I walked down the hallway, shaking in anticipation, there was an empty casket. The intensity of the moment was building, but I ran my hand along the edge of that casket. With that first direct contact with anything death-related, all my nervousness went away. They led me back to the embalming room and to the woman's body on the stainless-steel table.

"This is Mrs. Rowland. She died of an unexpected heart attack and was a wife, mother, and only daughter. It's important to keep in mind that this was a real person and be respectful."

He proceeded to inject the embalming fluid, explain the process, and answer my questions. It felt like a caring and vital process, and it didn't frighten me to imagine this as a career.

"So, what do you think?" Mom said. "Is this something you might want to do for a living?"

"Yes, definitely. It wasn't scary at all, and I learned a lot. What does it take to be a funeral director?"

"I'm sure you'll have to go to school to get a license."

There was that dreaded word—school. Maybe it will be a school where we just practice embalming and not be full of tests. It turned out to be a lot of science, psychology, accounting, and legal stuff, exactly what I had hoped to avoid for the rest of my life.

We researched mortuary programs and found a two-year program at the University of Minnesota. Mom wrote them for information, and they sent an application form and a test.

I thought, "I'll never get in. I can't do tests. And I have to write why I want to go into the funeral business." If I tell the truth, that I didn't think there would be tests and papers, just hands-on stuff, they really won't let me in.

I don't know if I accidentally picked the correct answers or if my mother changed my choices before returning the application, but in ten days, I received my acceptance letter. Everyone was excited and proud of me for being the first in my family to attend college, as if just going to college guaranteed a successful outcome. I was swept up in their excitement, but the nagging fear that I was going back to a world of failure lingered in my mind.

When the First A Changed My Life

## Chapter 8

I arrived at the University of Minnesota campus, eventually found my dorm, and moved in. I was proud to be a college student and determined to succeed, but everything was so new to me—stately buildings, people rushing everywhere, crowds wherever I went. And smiling students who looked like they knew what they were doing.

I wanted to do well and make my family proud, but deep down, I feared this would be another Mercy High, maybe worse. With such a dismal learning background, the only thing I knew about college was 'an hour out for every hour in' — that I would need to spend an hour studying for every hour of class time.

My heart sank as I browsed through the crowded university bookstore. The size of the textbooks was much bigger and more complex than anything I had encountered in high school. My hope faded, and the doubt that my good intentions were enough reappeared.

With my expensive textbooks sitting on my small dorm room desk, I went off to my first week of classes. I saw other students taking notes in class, and went back to the bookstore for the spiral-bound college notebooks. I did my best to record whatever the professor said and spent the necessary hour studying back in my room.

The first quarter grades were encouraging, low Bs and Cs, but they declined quarter by quarter. Classes in the third quarter included second and third classes in the science sequence, with new concepts flying at me at an overwhelming rate. The extra time didn't help, and my grades were low, with D's and one F, and I was put on academic probation.

When I returned the following fall, it was like they had changed the language. I couldn't understand what the professors were talking about, and the textbooks might as well have been in Greek. I gave it all I had, hoping some magic would happen, but every class I attended further confirmed that what I was doing didn't work. Within two weeks, I knew my days as a college student were over. I remember thinking, "I'm just not a college kid. I tried my best, and I can't learn what they are teaching."

It was more than discouragement. It was sadness over who I thought I might become and the realization that maybe this was all just pretending. I hoped there was something somewhere that would work for me. I just hadn't found it yet.

I didn't even bother to unenroll; I just walked away and moved into a small, converted garage apartment. Quitting wasn't just giving up. It felt like facing the truth—a painful, humiliating truth, but one that had been with me the whole time.

At the end of that quarter, the university sent my final grades, which were straight F's, to my parents. The letter said I had been dropped for low academic performance. My struggles and failures had repeated themselves, further disappointing my family. My mother, who had no clue that I was failing, sent me a note after receiving those final grades.

"One day, when you have children of your own, I hope you will experience the sadness and pain that I feel right now."

A mother's curse that deepened my shame beyond any I had ever felt in a classroom. I had failed and brought pain to my most ardent supporter. I was ashamed, and I had no excuse—it was just me, my fault. There was nothing I could do about it.

Fall came and went as I spent my days shipping packages for the Gold Bond Stamps company, and nights in my tiny, cold apartment, going over and over my life of failures. I seemed to be generating the grey fall clouds and causing the trees to give up their last leaves. Tormented by loneliness, I finally called Joe, an ex-classmate who had tried to help me in the anatomy class, and said, "I need some female companionship. Can you fix me up?"

He replied, "My girlfriend has a friend, but she's not a warm and friendly type. She's from England, and you might not get very far with her, if you know what I mean."

"I don't care. I just want a female to talk to, go to a movie, whatever. I'm desperate."

A week later, he picked me up. Sue, an attractive blonde with twinkling blue eyes, got into the car. I looked at her and smiled.

"I hear you are from England," I said. "My grandparents came from Ireland," hoping it was a bonding, common-ground statement.

"Oh no! Not another damn Irishman," were the first words she said to me.

Dumbfounded, I thought, *This is going to be a challenge.* I proceeded to charm her, telling stories and asking about her travels and adventures. We danced and talked throughout the evening, just what I needed.

I walked her to her door, as a charming gentleman would, and asked to see her again. I did, again and again, laughing together at English comedies, swatting mosquitoes around a small lake campfire, or having deep discussions about our futures. We married a year and a half later. I didn't tell her about my struggles with learning.

The day after the small ceremony in St. Paul, Minnesota, Sue and I packed everything into my twelve-year-old two-door Chevy. Off we went, headed West with $160, no job, no skills, no education, a history of failure, and not even a destination. We ate baloney sandwiches, slept in the car through thunderstorms in Kansas, stopping in Denver to work and save a bit more money.

We rented a semi-furnished duplex that included a table, chairs, and a mattress, along with a stove and refrigerator. I did some dumb things in those first days, calling her once, just once, by an old girlfriend's name. I also told her how to make the chicken gravy I remembered my mother making. My memory was so off that we had to throw the pan out.

The main carryover from my past was difficulty in making decisions. Here we were, twenty-one-year-old wanna-be grown-ups, and I hesitated to commit myself to even small decisions. I couldn't decide whether to ride or walk to a nearby park, which bus to take to the movie theater, or even which socks to buy for work. I just wasn't sure that I could make a good decision, the right decision.

I held back because I didn't want to be wrong in front of her. I didn't want her to think of me the way teachers and other students had throughout my past.

In the early days of our marriage, we fell into roles modeled by our parents, with the husband as the decision-maker and the wife the supportive spouse. It wasn't long before I found myself nervous about that role, and one evening I said. "I do not want to be the main decision-maker. I want this to be an equal marriage, a partnership where we share tasks and decisions."

But did I really want to give up that role? Would she see me as less of a man, respect me less? What if I make decisions and they are wrong? What will she think then? I didn't know how to be a good husband or a good partner.

If you say to a kid, "You're stupid!" once, it's not going to have much effect. But if you say it over and over again, for twelve years, it makes you doubt yourself, and it makes you believe what they say about you might be true. And that belief was now affecting my marriage and my life.

"I think I like this pink for the bathroom," Sue said, holding up the paint sample card.

"Naw, that's too bright. This light beige is better."

"That's dull and boring. You pick beige for everything. Pick something else."

She was right. Beige was my go-to color, safe and no risk-taking. How was I supposed to know if pink would look good? Or that bright blue? What if I picked this lime green and it was awful? I just couldn't decide.

"Whatever. You pick. I don't care."

"You can never make up your mind about anything. What's the matter with you?"

In my head, 'because I might be wrong' swirled around, and 'how do I know which choice is the right one?' If I make the wrong choice, you won't be happy, but if I don't make a choice, you will still be upset.

We bought an old oak rocking chair with a loose arm at a garage sale.

"Can you fix it?" Sue asked.

"I think so. Maybe just glue it. Shouldn't be hard."

I carried it into the garage, ready to get started, but I hesitated. Should I disassemble it? Or maybe glue and a nail? Maybe a screw would be better. A week went by, then another.

"When are you going to fix the rocking chair?

"I'm thinking about it. I can't decide the best way to do it. I might have to buy a clamp."

Another ten days later, I finally bought a clamp. It worked.

It was sitting in the living room when she came in. She said, "Finally! Why did it take so long?"

"I wanted to be sure the glue had dried."

But we both knew the truth: I was afraid of making the wrong decision.

## Chapter 9

It was Friday, and I had been stacking boards all week at the lumber yard where I worked. With hard work and minimal pay, it was still a struggle to pay the bills. Without any skills, it was the best I could get. I was tired of this, of life going nowhere.

We went to a friend's house for dinner that evening, and Toby said, "You are working with wood. Why don't you join the carpenters' union? Much better pay, and it's steady work. You just take a test to determine what level between apprentice and journeyman you are." Toby's suggestion was about to change my life, but I didn't know it yet.

"I don't do that well on tests." If he only knew what he was asking of me.

"It's a test about construction, not names and dates. I have the study guide, and you can have it. The test is mainly pictures for you to label. Worth a shot."

*Maybe it is. Anything is worth changing what I'm doing.*

The study guide was about house and commercial construction, with lots of illustrations, and I could imagine myself working on those job sites. It felt good to imagine where the board in my hand might end up.

At the lumberyard, I thought about the test as I handled the lumber. Maybe it would not be the same as before. This test is about real things, not just words in a book.

"You do like working with your hands, and it is connected to what you do now. I think you should try," Sue said. "You'll do fine on the test."

With a dry mouth and a shaky stomach, I walked through the dusty glass front door of the union hall, about to face one more test.

*Please let this be different.*

The old carpenter giving the test welcomed me and was friendly, and calmly said, "Here is the test. You can sit at that table and take as long as you'd like. Let me know when you've finished."

This was certainly different from the school tests that carried a message of failure. This was a test of things I had touched, things I had done, either physically or in my mind. I was at a table by myself, not in a desk surrounded by students who would get all the answers right, while I cringed with the shame of not knowing. It was still a bit scary—but it didn't feel hopeless.

He scored it while I waited, and that took just a few minutes.

"Congratulations! You passed with flying colors," he said, as he reached out to shake my hand.

"Come here to the union hall Monday morning, and they will get you signed up. You start at the bottom of the list, but as the jobs come in, you'll move up. You should be on a job within ten days or so."

Nervous and excited, I tossed and turned that night, thinking about the good that was coming—no tests, working with my hands, more money, and a real skill. Not just a laborer, but becoming a capable and professional carpenter. Little did I know the real benefit—discovering that learning was not beyond me after all.

The first job I went on was the Shell Oil Refinery in Walnut Creek, California, where I was among the hundred or so journeymen carpenters. We built complex forms to hold the concrete foundations and pillars that would support the pipes of flowing oil. I watched, asked questions, and tried to anticipate what the experienced carpenters would need or do next.

I learned that if your handsaw hits a nail, it will cut crooked from then on. And I hit my finger so many times with a hammer that I thought the bruises would never go away, but I was learning a skill, a trade that would support my family and that I could be proud of. I had no trouble learning how to use a square or hold a chalk line tight enough to snap a straight line.

There were no exams or grades; all I needed to do was work hard, measure accurately, cut straight, and carry my end of the board. I was judged by what I did, not by what I had read and failed to recite correctly. The classroom had seen me as lacking; the job site showed I could be excellent.

Bill, a no-nonsense, hard-working journeyman, and I were working on a form for a pillar that would eventually hold the main structure. I watched carefully to see how he would handle the complex angles, and I tried to figure out what he would do next. When I saw he was about to need the saw, another tool, or a material, I would place it next to him.

He started to say, "Hand me the...," when he saw it was right there. He looked up at me, then the board, and went back to work. Soon, he quit asking and just reached for the part he needed, knowing it would be waiting for him. The job went quickly, and when finished, he stood up, looked at me, and said, "Gotta tell you. You are the best apprentice I've worked with in my 27 years. You think ahead, and you keep things moving, and every day there is a fight over who gets you for a partner."

No teacher had ever spoken to me like that. I was beginning to think I was more than what the school world thought I was.

Being valued by those I looked up to, who wanted me working alongside them and had taught me nearly everything I knew about carpentry, drove away the clouds of failure that had followed me. Carpentry was always about getting the entire job finished, and that gave me an understanding of where my task fit in the process. I was learning, and it felt good.

One rainy day in September, the crew was sitting in the carpenter's shack eating lunch and telling stories. Someone would comment on dropping his hammer from two stories up. The next guy would top that with how he had lost his entire toolbox over the edge of a six-story building.

"It spread my tools over half a block. Some I never found."

"First liar doesn't stand a chance," Dan quipped, with a smile. Dan, a crusty old guy with a Texas drawl, was the foreman with 30-plus years in the trade.

The conversation shifted to their lives as carpenters, jobs they'd worked on, and how there is always more work in an election year. Dan pointed to me and said, "He's going to be our boss someday." The eight experienced, professional journeymen carpenters all nodded in agreement.

"What?" I said, dumbfounded.

Dan said, "I've been in the business my entire life, and I've seen leaders come and go. I know what I'm talking about. You have it, whatever 'it' is. You are going to end up the boss."

Could that be true? What did he see in me? I started watching how Dan led the crew, resolved issues, and gave clear, careful instructions. I thought, "I could do that." Maybe Father Martin was wrong about me being a leader.

After I had been a carpenter for maybe a year, my wife asked me to do some honey-do thing around the house.

I was halfway through the task when she came over, watching for a minute before saying,

"What happened to you? You used to take so long before you'd start anything. Now, whatever it is, you jump right in."

I paused, taken aback. I hadn't realized the shift until she named it. She was right—without even noticing it, I'd stopped hesitating. The carpenter in me had learned to trust his hands, and the doubt that once froze me was slipping away.

Before learning to be a carpenter, I doubted I could do anything correctly. That doubt was always there, whispering in my ear that I'd screw it up, that someone else could do it better, faster, cleaner. Whatever the job was, whether hanging a picture or fixing the screen door, I had to look and think, worry and doubt my solutions. I put it off so I wouldn't make a mistake.

The carpenter experience gradually gave me the confidence to see how something should be done and how to get right in and do it. That's what you have to do on the job, and it carried over into my home life. It was a shock for me to realize that I had learned a lot, and it wasn't even that hard.

*What else might I be able to learn? Why is carpentry so easy for me? What has changed?*

What struck me was that my wife had noticed the old version of me, the hesitant and doubting boy. She had no way of knowing the turmoil inside of me. She had seen the version of me I'd worked hard to leave behind. And somehow, even seeing that part of me, she didn't turn away. I felt embarrassed and loved.

## When the First A Changed My Life

One late summer day, we took our five-year-old daughter, Susie, to enroll her in the nearby two-room schoolhouse. One of the last remaining pioneer schools, it originally was for first through eighth grades but now holds only first and second. Mrs. Deardorff, her first-grade teacher, welcomed us warmly. We completed the paperwork, and as we left, she said, "You are welcome anytime to stop by to see how we teach."

I took her at her word. One afternoon, a few weeks later, when the construction job was halted by rain, I showed up at the door, kicked off my muddy boots, and came in to watch my wonderful daughter. I found an empty chair and sat in the corner to watch the teacher and kids interact. That didn't last long.

Mrs. Deardorff handed me a small storybook and asked, "Would you read this to that group of girls?" We gathered in a corner and, sitting on a rug, I read to them as I had often read to Susie before bedtime. For fun, I changed the names of the characters in the story to the kids' names, and they were fully engrossed in the tale.

At the end of the school day, I stood by the door with Mrs. Deardorff as the kids filed out to board the waiting school bus. One of the girls from the reading group stopped and gave me a big hug, a nice surprise. After the kids were gone, Mrs. Deardorff said, "That girl who hugged you lost her father last summer, and there are several others who have no dad at home. We need more men teaching in elementary." The seed was planted.

I returned every chance I could to help kids learn to make their letters or listen to the show-and-tell stories. Once, I paired up with a tiny boy, bright-eyed but shy, to help him with the Go Dog Go book, a favorite of my daughter. As he struggled with even these simple lines, I could see his embarrassment, and I realized, "This is me. I know what that look on his face means, what he is feeling." All of the memories of the exasperated tone of the teacher and the look-away glances of other kids flooded back.

He was not going to get that from me! I praised him for trying so hard, for good guesses, and for telling me about his dog at home. The more I praised his effort, the harder he tried, and he soon made progress with reading the words.

For the rest of the time I was there, and no matter what he was doing, he looked to me for that encouragement. Across the room, I could see him struggle with something, get frustrated, and look up at me. I would give him a thumbs-up, he would smile, and go back to work.

The realization shook me to my core—my small interactions were truly shaping his life. I could see myself in him, desperately searching for that same thumbs-up in school, that approval that never came. And in that moment, a thought surfaced that I couldn't ignore: *Maybe I should be a teacher.*

That thought pounded in my head for days, until I brought up the idea with Mrs. Deardorff. Her response startled me.

"You are great with kids. I've been hoping that you would consider being a teacher."

With that encouragement, I asked Sue, "Do you think I could be a teacher?"

"You are a teacher already. I see it with our girls, and in the stories you tell about what you do at the school. All you need is the license."

That began the process of filling out applications, exploring financial aid, and weighing the impact of moving, until the day the acceptance letter arrived. I packed up my carpenter tools and bought the clothes I thought a twenty-nine-year-old college student should wear.

The drive to help the confused and beaten-down kids drove the fear of failure out of my head, right until I arrived on the Illinois State University campus.

When the First A Changed My Life

# Chapter 10

I wandered the Illinois State University campus in a daze.

*What the hell am I doing here? This is not going to work. I've never been able to do this. Never!*

It was the fall of 1969, and the day of my first quiz, twelve questions covering the concepts in the beginning chapter of Psychology 101.

*The argument in my head was relentless:*
"You're going to fail."
"But I studied—really studied this time."

## When the First A Changed My Life

*"You never passed a test in your life! Remember high school? Remember the University of Minnesota?"*

As I climbed the steps to the classroom, I couldn't talk to anyone, couldn't look at anyone. I could overhear the comments as the real students, the eighteen-year-olds with outstanding grades, teacher's pets, every last one of them. They were talking about last night's date, what they want for lunch, and that stuff they call music.

*I don't belong here.*

I filed in and found my seat as the instructor said, "The quiz is on your desk, face down. Don't turn it over until I say so." I sat there with my eyes closed.

I had tried. I read and reread the chapter. I went to class and took notes. I studied at home and reviewed everything early this morning. I've never been this ready, but still...

"Begin! You have twenty minutes."

With trembling hands, I turned the quiz over, read the dozen questions, and burst into tears. The instructor, dismayed to see this thirty-year-old man in the midst of the class of eighteen-year-olds, sobbing into his hands, patted me gently on the shoulder. He said softly, "Easy now. It's just a quiz."

That moment didn't come out of nowhere. Fear had been building since I first set foot on the campus.

A couple of weeks earlier, it was the September orientation week. I was enrolled as a freshman majoring in elementary education, and wandered around the campus, trying to take it all in. My hands shook, and I was breathing fast. I was scared. I told everybody in any casual conversation that came up that I was married, had kids, and working part-time. I would take classes, then probably drop out for a while to earn more money.

## When the First A Changed My Life

*If I fail, I'll just say I had to drop out to work—no harm, no shame.*

I walked from the bookstore with an armload of textbooks that were much heavier than anything I had carried in high school. I caught up with a guy who had sat behind a table at orientation, stopped to say hi and tell him my story.

I don't know whether he saw my fear in my eyes or was just being generally helpful, but he said, "On the third floor of Stevenson Hall, there's a study skills center. They talk about note-taking and speed reading, maybe save you some time."

I stepped off the sidewalk and walked straight past the Do Not Walk On The Grass sign to Stevenson Hall as fast as I could with my armload of books. I never knew such a place existed.

I was again telling my story to the young college student behind the desk when a small, grey-haired woman touched my arm. She introduced herself as Dr. Leslie Carlton, director of the Study Skill

Center. I followed her to her office, where she asked what I needed and how I studied.

"How do you study a chapter in a textbook?"

"I start at the beginning and read the chapter, usually more than once, and try to remember what it said."

"What do you do when you go to class?"

"Find a seat in the back of the room, and try to write down whatever the professor says, at least what I hope are the main points. Usually, it's all going too fast. I know I miss stuff. And the next day, I barely remember any of it."

Something about her demeanor, her warm, accepting tone, and the gentleness of her questions led me to pour out the failures I thought I had buried, along with the crushing fear that it would happen again.

I laid out my string of academic failures, my life as a husband and father, and my work as a carpenter. She pointed out the advanced learning and problem-solving that I had demonstrated outside of school.

One of the main points she made was that I have been learning my whole life. Everything that I know from people that I have met, how to identify objects and skills at work, how to drive a car, and the millions of other things, was all evidence that I actually did learn.

Her concluding message nearly exploded my heart, "You have been trying to learn as the majority learns, but you learn differently. It's okay to learn your own way, as you have done with great success."

Mom was right when she said, "You are just different, and that's OK."

Now, I was in a place that could help me identify how I learn and how to refine and apply those skills in an academic world. The problem wasn't that I couldn't learn, but that I had been taught wrong.

*"To learn as I learn"* became my mantra for believing in myself. That, along with specific note-taking techniques and a systematic approach to learning, set me afire. Whoever that stranger on the

sidewalk was, that angel was instrumental in setting me on a path that changed my life.

At the Study Skills Center, I gained skills in notetaking, speed-reading, test preparation, and a variety of other effective study practices. I went five days a week, every spare moment, to learn as much as I could about how learning takes place.

With help from Dr. Carlton, I discovered that I learn holistically: once I see the big picture, the details fall into place, forming an easy-to-remember, single, interconnected whole. She taught me study strategies that supported my way of learning. The typical approach of accumulating facts to reach a conclusion and finally understand the concept just never worked for me. I could now understand my struggles in those early conflicts with schooling, and both relief and hope emerged.

For the first time in my life, I had an actual strategy for studying, including what to do when I had a textbook chapter to read. I had always read it as if I were reading a novel. You just read, start to finish, and try to remember it all. Alternate approaches to reading a chapter fit my way of learning. For the first time, concepts became clear and understandable.

I didn't know there were strategies that would help you learn the material. In a basic psychology class, I put those strategies to use. I surveyed the book, read the information, wrote down questions, drew mind maps, wrote down answers, reviewed them, and spoke them out loud.

Then came the first Illinois State University quiz. Here I was, a graduate in the lower tenth of my high school class. Flunked out of college. I tried as hard as I knew how, but nothing had worked. I had walked away, quit school for good. And it's now ten years later, and I'm back among the fresh-faced students. I couldn't help but believe I would repeat the shame of the hundreds of failed quizzes.

*The instructor put his hand on my shoulder and quietly said, "Easy now. It's just a quiz."*

I look up at him with tears still flowing and try to speak. For a few seconds, I could only shake my head.

"No, no, no. You don't understand." I picked up the paper that represented the now broken barrier, and, between choking sobs, said, "I know all this. All of it. I know it all."

What he couldn't hear was the string of thoughts that rushed through my head:

*I know this. I am capable. I am going to graduate.*

*I am going to succeed. I CAN learn!*

At that moment, that instant, my life changed.

As much as I wanted to succeed, inside, I was sure I would repeat the hundreds of failed quizzes in my educational life. Instead, I discovered the truth — my years of doubt about my ability to learn were wrong.

As I applied the study strategies taught at the Study Skills Center and developed more of my own, I became curious about why they were working. In other classes, learning instantly became easy, and I wanted to know why.

When teachers started with vocabulary lists and names to memorize, it felt like being handed a box of nails without knowing what I was supposed to build. But once I understood the framework of a concept, the details fell into place naturally. Facts finally had a place to belong. Recalling them was just a matter of walking through the concept from whole to part.

With the aggressive-reading techniques, the old adage of an hour out for every hour in fell by the wayside. I could take a whole chapter of a college textbook, a week's assignment, and read, take notes, and review it, all in 15 minutes. Learning became effortless. The results were passing every quiz, every test with high scores. I thought about what I had almost missed, and about others who, although capable, never find the answer to their "Why" question.

The final course grades for a Sociology 101 class were posted on the cork bulletin board outside the professor's office. Students were crowded around the computer printout, vying for a spot to check how well they did. As I walked up to that list of student IDs and grades, I hoped it would be, at best, a C, sure that it was what I deserved.

I scanned the list of grades.

There it was—an F. My stomach lurched.

Failed again! I knew it! I hung my head and started to turn away.

But then—wait. That's not my student ID.

I ran my finger further down the list, searching for my own ID. When I finally found it, I blinked hard and shook my head. Next to it—an A.

I took a step back as other students crowded around the grade sheet. I leaned in again, pulling out my student ID to double-check my number. I traced the line over to the grade. It was still an A.

The thought that I, the student with so many years of terrible grades, would ever do better than a C was deeply ingrained. When I saw the A, there was a flash thought, "He made a mistake. This can't be my grade." But I mentally retraced every paper, quiz, and test, the careful work I had done, and the new study strategies that supported how I learn. Slowly, the truth struggled to the surface.

*I, John Tenny, am an A student.*

Ten years earlier, I left the academic world, with proof that I just wasn't smart enough to be in college, confirmed by the prior twelve years of F's and D's. The colors around me brightened as a wave of warmth flowed from head to foot. I locked my fingers on top of my head and stared at that single line, that single letter, as the doubt I had worn like a second skin faded away.

That A, now on my permanent record at Illinois State University, was the proof that I could learn. The newly discovered study strategies let my way of learning surge forward and beat back the years of shame. The A was more than a grade – it was the open door to my future.

I walked down the hall and through the sunlit doorway and started down the sidewalk. In a few minutes, I found myself back at the front door. In a daze, I had walked in a circle, back to the building that held the symbol, the proof that I was worthy after all.

I thought back to the days and years of repeated shame and the feeling of giving up for what I believed was the final time. The memories—the teacher's "This is all wrong. Do it over," the scorn and sneers of other students, my mother's sigh of disappointment at every report card—all proof that I couldn't learn, that something was wrong with me—rose to the surface. I could feel myself turning and stepping away from that past.

Life is different now. *I can learn.*

As I walked across campus, eager to share with my family that their belief in me had been justified,

I felt myself stepping into the future no one—least of all I—ever imagined would be mine. Ahead lay years of rising confidence, honors, degrees, and leadership in teaching. But I wasn't envisioning any of that—I only saw that the world of learning was mine, in a future no longer ruled by doubt.

# Epilogue

Over fifty-five years ago, I turned over that first quiz and felt what once was unthinkable: I know this. I still choke up when I think about the timid boy who suffered for those twelve years. He believed he was incapable, only to discover he was not only capable but talented. I mourn the years lost, but in the end thankful that I found my way.

That moment didn't delete my past, but it charged my future. Self-doubt, once the cloud through which I viewed everything, faded. I had believed that learning was some magic others possessed. Instead, I discovered that my mind worked wonderfully—just different. Once I understood that, the skies opened.

I loved my years as a carpenter. They grounded me, taught me to watch, to plan, to act. But stopping there would have meant living a smaller version of myself. Experiencing that physical learning gave me the courage to risk something bigger. It gave me the confidence to become a student again, then a teacher, then someone who could help others find what I had spent so long searching for. The doubt that lingers, as it always does, is now about the quality of my decisions rather than my ability to make them.

I didn't recognize my strengths for many years, even when others named them—leadership, insight, the ability to connect and guide. I turned those comments away, sure that they belonged to someone else. Later, I stepped into leadership not to command, but to lift. I wanted to give students, teachers, and colleagues the sense of worth I had once needed so badly.

If only Mom could see me now. I'd want her to know that I recognize the depth of her mother's love and all that I owe her. Mrs. Dearforff, carpenter foreman Dan, Dr. Carlton, and the stranger on the sidewalk—every one of them guided me on my path. I hope I've done the same for others. That is my true measure of success.

If you picked up this book because doubt has shadowed your life, I hope you have seen yourself somewhere in these pages. I hope you recognize that your struggle, your fear and failures say nothing about your capacity. You are not alone in your confusion or frustration. You are not the labels you were given. You are not the sum of old wounds. You are not finished.

# When the First A Changed My Life

# Afterword

This story has been nagging me for decades. I graduated in the lowest 10% of my high school class, yet eventually earned a Ph.D. I taught in the public schools and built a career that culminated in directing a graduate school of education and being inducted into the Illinois State University Hall of Fame. Even so, my early struggles with school and learning never fully left me. I have questioned how my success could ever have happened, and over time, understood why. It wasn't about my abilities—it was about the lingering self-doubt and the effect of early labeling.

This is not a book about awards or credentials. It is about what happens when someone comes to believe they are not capable, and how long that belief can last. I wrote this for those who have been labeled and have believed that defines them. It is for those who see themselves by what they can't do, and are blind to their broader abilities. And for anyone who still carries the weight of self-doubt, even after life shows them otherwise.

Looking back now, I can see the cost of not understanding how I learned. Confused parents and teachers interpreted my actions as inadequate and conveyed that message to a young, developing child. I believed that when learning was hard, it was my fault—that something was wrong with me.

What no one, including me, could see was the conflict between how I learn and how they taught. I was fully capable of learning, but I narrowed my efforts to learn in ways that didn't fit how my mind works. Using their measure of success brought on the fear and shame that blocked my ability to see my potential. In that world, I struggled just to survive and endure—and that's never enough.

For most students, the school system works well. For others—equally capable—it does not.

Learning differences are not learning deficits. The differences are in how meaning is built, how patterns are recognized, how understanding takes shape.

The problem wasn't that I couldn't learn. It was that I was expected to learn as others did—not how I learn, how my brain works.

What eventually helped was not more effort, but a different approach. I learned best when I could see the whole before the parts—when structure came before detail, and meaning before memorization. Once I understood the framework, the details were all interconnected and had somewhere to land, and a path for recalling. Before that, they simply faded away. For me, and others like me, starting from the structure makes tracing the path to the details easy.

When learning became easy, I was first surprised, then curious to find out what was happening in my brain. I spent a lot of effort learning about how the brain works and how that might be applied to learning in school. That led to developing specific strategies, yielding quick and dependable learning tools. The journey became this memoir, and the tools became the basis for years of teaching capable and struggling students.

Even now, doubt returns from time to time. It is not as harsh as it once was, but it hasn't vanished entirely. That surprised me. I assumed success would silence it for good. Instead, I've learned that doubt often signals growth—another moment when old tools no longer fit. I'm now aware of self-doubt, and I look to see if I'm doubting my ability or the quality of my decision. I'll never know my ability unless I try. Doubting the quality of decisions leads to better decisions. Asking why something isn't working opens more doors than deciding I can't. A label is a description of what I can't do and ignores the rest of me — what I can do.

Capability is real. It exists even when it goes unrecognized, even when it is buried beneath doubt or fear. Understanding yourself—how you learn, how you make sense of the world—changes what becomes possible.

John L Tenny

Life eventually led me into decades of teaching, studying how learning takes place, and helping others find approaches that fit them better than the ones they were given. It's been a satisfying life.

My story ends here.
Yours does not.

*Our doubts are traitors and make us lose the good we often might win, by fearing to attempt.*
--William Shakespeare

John L Tenny

# Author and Study Resources

Visit John's Author page,
teaching resources, and study tools.

———————————————

Send John a note—*he reads every message.*

LearningPathPress@gmail.com
Author ° Speaker ° Study Tools

———————————————

Sixteen Study Strategies

*"For every learner who thought they were behind—
your breakthrough is closer than you think."*

John L Tenny

www.ingramcontent.com/pod-product-compliance
Lightning Source LLC
Chambersburg PA
CBHW030448100526
44580CB00002B/31